DEAR LIFE

By Dennis O'Driscoll

Dennis O'Driscoll

Dear Life

ANVIL PRESS POETRY

Published in 2012
by Anvil Press Poetry Ltd
Neptune House 70 Royal Hill London SE10 8RF
www.anvilpresspoetry.com

This book is published with financial assistance
from Arts Council England

Designed and set in Minion by Anvil
Printed and bound in Great Britain
by Hobbs the Printers Ltd

ISBN 978 0 85646 446 1

A catalogue record for this book
is available from the British Library

God made everything out of nothing,
but the nothingness shows through.

— PAUL VALÉRY

ACKNOWLEDGEMENTS

Acknowledgements are due to the following, where some of the poems in this collection were published or broadcast: *Alaska Quarterly Review*, *American Poetry Review*, *Best of Irish Poetry 2010* (edited by Matthew Sweeney, Southword Editions), *Boulevard Magenta*, *The Dark Horse*, *Five Points*, *Hampden-Sydney Poetry Review*, *The Irish Times*, *Narrative*, *New Ohio Review*, *The New Republic*, *The New Yorker*, *The Poetry Paper* (Aldeburgh Poetry Festival), *Poetry Review*, *RTE Radio 1*, *Shine On* (edited by Pat Boran, Dedalus Press), *Southword*, *The Spectator*, *The Stony Thursday Book* and *TriQuarterly*. 'Museum' was written in response to a commission from Paddy Ryan and the committee of the Revenue Museum, Dublin. Profound thanks to J. Patrick Lannan and the Lannan Foundation (New Mexico) for their support and encouragement. The assistance of An Chomhairle Ealaíon/The Arts Council is also gratefully acknowledged.

CONTENTS

Dear Life

YESTERDAY

Been there.
Done that.

Digested the three
requisite meals.

Reacted with
appropriate outrage

to whatever headlined
controversies there were.

The dead took no hand,
act or part.

The children of the future
made no demands.

Its like will not
be seen again.

Those of us alive then
had the whole world

to ourselves.
The whole livelong day.

SUB

And if, from the get-go, life were touted
like a magazine subscription, would you –
knowing what you do now – sign up?

Take the six-month trial ('Money back if not satisfied')?
Tick the 'Yes, please' box?
The 'Rush me' one with the 'Bill me later' option?

Or would you sit on your calloused hands,
refusing all inducements, declining
the introductory gifts, the easy terms
available to new subscribers?
Sit there, lend your name to nothing?

That warm morning, saved like a lock
of ungreying hair, when you dragged
a stiff kitchen chair to the garden,
the gold-embossed blue cover
of your school library classic
matching the hyacinth-blue wrapper
of the Cadbury's chocolate bar
you'd stocked for later pleasure.

That blackbird whose voice
was recognisable from the old
monastic poem penned
in the margin of a vellum page.

That observant lake: logging every detail,
poring over every movement,
taking an impress of the morning
like the credit card of a hotel guest
at the check-in desk.

That moment in summer when
butterflies re-enter your orbit:
package tourists bounding
through Arrivals in Hawaiian shirts.
The dipstick iridescence of a dragonfly.

✳

You know well you'd end up
pretending to hover over the boxes
before ticking 'Send no further offers'
or the one starkly marked 'No, thanks'.
Then get on with your life.

FABRICATIONS

God is dead to the world.

But he still keeps up
          appearances. Day after
day he sets out his stall.
          Today, his special is

a sun-melt served on
          a fragrant bed of
moist cut-grass; yesterday,
          a misty-eyed moon,

a blister pack of stars.
          Lakes and mountains
are standard stock;
          flowers and birds

in season. The avocado,
          shining knight, and the
tightly-swathed cabbage
          remain evergreens.

Odd years, for novelty,
          he tweaks the weather
patterns, brings forward
          spring by weeks, lets

the crocus's petal-
          pronged attack on
frozen ground begin
          ahead of schedule:

softening air's frosty
      disposition; making good
the winter's blemishes.
      Special effects – flash floods,

meteor showers clashing
      overhead, the cradle cap
of a lunar eclipse – are reserved
      for visionary interludes.

Not that it matters;
      nothing is sacred anymore;
no one much takes him
      at his word, buys his

version of the story, seeks
      corroboration of his
claims; the steeple's beak
      no longer nourishes its flock.

People idly browse his wares,
      knock back samples
of coconut milk, add Gruyère
      to a quiche, test the texture

of the beach sand with bare feet,
      before resorting to the soft
option of a recliner: a pew from
      which to worship the sun's heat.

Blowing hot or cold
      as mood or precedent
dictates, he offers further
      cryptic clues – a flatfish

sporting two left eyes,
  a tree that moults fur catkins,
an orchid mimicking a fly,
  a blackbird whose bill

is toucan orange, a baby battling
  with acute leukaemia,
a cow resting among buttercups
  like a whale awash in plankton.

But few make the link,
  speculate enough
to track these fabrications
  back to source.

He starts from scratch each day
  with new creations: drafting
a summer dawn, he permits
  the sun – only minimally

resisted by the mist, a token
  skirmish – to assume control,
making for profligate horizons,
  lofty skies, beyond which

other universes stack up,
  dangled in suspense,
the way a mountain lake
  is cupped in sandstone hands.

And every pulsing star will live
  according to his lights,
individually illumined,
  nimbus visible to the eye.

AT REST

Even the most burdened of businessmen –
time is money merchants – are out for
the count, paying the price for switching off
in favour of the weightless state of sleep
by giving up each night's potential output
gratis, like the takings of a benefit gig.

Happy as the night is long, dreamers
revert to a primitive stance and – working
components flipped to standby mode –
heave steady breaths like sighs of relief,
snort the addictive air. Slack penises relax
at half mast, a complete flop, breasts level off.

Equality officers, hedge-fund speculators,
lap dancers, rubber tappers lay down
their lives, defenceless against the night's
inexorable threats, naked or attired in flannel
bedwear, stripped of rank. Can evolution
not dispense with this primeval throwback?

Why – buttressed with labour-saving devices
though their existences may be – are the most
upright citizens brought to the brink of collapse
at the tail-end of every day; nothing less
than this comatose opt-out between duvets,
sheets meeting human recuperation needs?

And they regain consciousness reluctantly,
never as refreshed as they'd envisaged,
the startled faces in the bathroom glass

unshaved, unmade-up, unreconciled,
moon-pale and drawn as ever, sleep
always failing to put off the evil day.

SPARE US

Spare us the spring.
Spare us its garish light.
Spare us the nerve-thumping
rhythms of hopping balls:
empty vessels, sterile leather eggs.

Spare us the false optimism,
the short-term vision, the hint
that winter has been dealt a fatal blow,
that days will keep on stretching,
an economy in boom.

Spare us the emotion of
the choked-up lawnmower
champing at resurgent grass.

And spare us, no less, the need
for wonder: it demands
too much suspension of belief.

Spare us our jaundiced view
of daffodils, those clichéd ingénues
that wizen limply into spineless stalks.

Spare us the shivering snowdrops,
paling quickly to insignificance,
their holier-than-thou aura
melting like Communion hosts.

Spare us the scare tactics
of invading dandelions,
that urine splash from which

no clump of grass,
no roadside verge is safe.

Lump in the leaves – it will be left to us
to pick up their pieces, rummage
through their trash when the tree market
crashes and stocks are in freefall.

And spare us lilacs, scent so over-ripe
suspicion of some cover-up is strong.

Spare us the lambs – bouncing
with complete abandon, needing
no counsel of a *carpe diem* nature,
peeking from the milk-white fleece
of their mothers' blanket coverage,
or savouring mint-green grass
– on whom we pin dark,
raddle-marked declarations of intent.

Spare us the ardent couples
conferring at the paint store, torn
conspiratorially between Dewberry Frost
emulsion and velvet-finish Moonlight Bay.

Spare us the bees raiding every flower in sight,
leaving no anther pocket unturned.
And the tantrum-throwing wasps,
in venomous mood, headbutting glass.

Spare us the spurned bird, egg on its face,
its singsong persistence in soliciting a mate,
its loutish whistling at wing-batting females.

And spare us the dawn chorus
that outwears its welcome
like a loquacious breakfast guest.

Spare us, therefore, the spring,
its fake sincerity, its unethical
marketing strategies, its deceptive
pledges, its built-in obsolescence,
its weeds breeding like flies.

CANUTE

I rush to bring this incoming seawater to heel

to check a new wave of aggression
    warn formally against excessive force
decree that the ocean should sign and seal –
    with its inimitable blue flourish – a binding protocol
on the territorial limits of its influence

I venture to take the waters by storm
    restraining their worst instincts
for conquest the destructive tendency they'd shown
    in pulverising strands with centuries
of foaming foul-mouthed pounding

the time has come to put a marker down
    stand firm against this restless
viscous trembling mess – too long pandered to –
    that slithers past my boundary walls
with brine-borne contraband

meltwater clear though my demands are
    insurgent waves still pillage
mustering superior forces for invasion
    I will maintain my singleminded vigil
curb spillage that seeks more than its own level

and spells bad tidings for whatever dry land may remain

THE SUNDAY GAME

How alive, how excitable
        they were back then,
when they congregated
        in the neighbour's kitchen
for the Sunday game:
        the one neighbour with TV.

Every spot is occupied: painted form,
        squat milking stool, squeaky
Morris Minor seat, with vinyl trim,
        reincarnated as a sofa.
They get stuck in: loud wheezy cheers,
        blunt denunciations of the ref...

Tension so immense that if
        a Cathay Pacific jumbo chanced
to touch down on the dung-plated
        sun-saturated farmyard
not one would cast a living
        glance in its direction.

Except, that is, the woman of
        the house: she lifts the kettle off
the hob again, fills it from a shaded
        bucket, the summer-blistered
hall door open to all comers.
        No questions asked.

COMPO

Be absolutely apoplectic.
Fuming mad.
Lobby. Picket. Hector.
Threaten to bring your case
to the highest tribunal in the land.
Demand a proper compensation package.
Counselling. A confidential help-line.
Throw a tantrum. Go ballistic.
Let them know what rage is.
Insist on full transparency. Accountability.
It's just not good enough in this day and age.
Independent experts have shown.
Leading consultants proved.
Hold out for answers for however long it needs.
Draw the line.
Give dog's abuse.
Call for the politicians to do something.
Get off their fat arses for once.
There's simply no excuse.
It should all have been foreseen in the upper echelons.
They haven't heard the last.
No way.
Someone has to take the rap.
You're fed up to the teeth.
Won't stand their crap one minute longer.
Heads must roll.

LAST STAND

God gets nothing right these days,
our ways no longer his ways.
Growing in number, boldness,
his antagonists, planning his overthrow,
refuse to let him stand on ceremony.

Preaching the gospel of human autonomy,
cosmologists supply creation
with a rational basis, a credible pedigree,
a back story, obviate the need for
divine intervention, miracle solutions.

Those consecrated to his cause
were cheated of their lives,
wasting their sweet intentions
on the desert fathers' airs.

Those who feared his might
recoiled from a mere figment
of their warped imaginations.

Brown-robed monks, tonsured heads
crammed with nonsense about eternity,
who spewed out orisons in concert,
were simply amusing themselves,
plainchanting inanely like
their enclosed communities of bees.

Calligraphic scribes, living by
his vision, wringing colour from
his precious stones for pigment,

hanging on to every facet of his word,
illuminating his script, observing
his declarations to the letter,
were no better than doodlers:
wet-day children amused
with a colouring book.

Nuns in wind-chastened mountain
convents, averting eyes from the world,
were victims of a confidence trickster;
virgins of whom he took advantage shamelessly.

The faithful, intoning rosaries in lakeside
retreat houses – bequeathed in his honour
by pious, misguided devotees – were left
addressing high, drystone, whitewashed walls.

His time has come to do the decent thing:
throw in the blood-soaked towel, abdicate
his throne, bow out finally, allowing the will
of the long-suffering majority to prevail.

Impossible to pin down, he has fallen
as silent as the infinite spaces
that rendered Pascal mute:
gaps unplugged in the universe.
Silent as the contemplative order
sedated in the terminal ward.
Silent as the tongues of dusty shoes
dumbfounded in the Holocaust Museum.

His era has ended.
Truly free at last
to pursue the good life

without his spoilsport
interference – not cast
as baddie always,
stigmatised with guilt,
browbeaten to confess –
you are absolved of every sin.
Now let thy earthly will be done.

TABLET X

[GILGAMESH]

Life, ruthless boss, lays us off
without protective notice.
Contracts strictly short-term.
Not one position permanent.

Uprooted from whatever
plot we try to make our
own, we are tossed away
like brittle reeds: there

one second, then – *snap*
– downgraded to the playthings
of a random breeze.
The personable young woman

amassing a high-achiever CV,
defying talk of a glass ceiling;
the raring-to-go young man,
beginning to hit his stride:

they lose ground in time,
caught in a downward slide
of degeneration and decline,
net contributors no longer.

ᘏ

And yet we flail about –
signing up for reiki treatments,
touting for new business,
doctoring mortgage forms,

labouring over garage
conversion plans, testing
missiles, feathering nests,
threatening neighbours with the full rigour –

when all the indications are
we are not long for this world:
waste water; sluice gate
froth thrown overboard.

Our mayfly existence –
one-day wonder – is done with
in a flutter, the current
registering no loss, ironing

out its ripples like a girl
smoothing a wrinkled skirt.
Death is the very spit
of life, its flip side: see

how alike they are –
those dead and those
asleep – when the former
repose on the mortuary slab.

Your survival is at
the pleasure of the gods,
their whim, your itinerary
plotted right to the final stop.

They it was who sanctioned
your first gasp of breath.
As for when you may
anticipate your last

and let death have its day,
their lips are sealed like
coffin lids, the whited
sepulchres of mighty kings.

TASKMASTERS

Now that your nose is to the cornerstone,
you'll stay the course, top off each block
with slops of mortar, bring down the trowel's
iron discipline like a ton of bricks.
And soon you're in the swing of things,
absorbed by what you'd dreaded,
content as someone settling in a train,
aromatic latte in hand, newspaper
and glossy mag secured underarm,
moist caesar salad sandwich in reserve
behind protective cellophane –
an emergency lever encased in glass.

                    ✍

Spring's surge of hormonal urgency
has long abated as you succumb
to ennui, wondering what you'd
ever seen in that hyperactive season.
Winter's scorched-earth policy takes hold
with a vengeance now, killing off everything
unable to fight back through hardy networks
of roots, brutal bare-knuckle thorns.
Snow flaking from damp walls of cloud,
the ascendant moon assuming pole position,
you abandon every pretence at outdoor
chores, build up defences from
the stockade of logs – the past year's
hatchet jobs – you'd laid in for
the open fireplace of your tied cottage.
You might decide to sketch out plans

for next summer's borders, browse
online catalogues of exotic shrubs.
But chances are you'll just lounge there
on the leather couch, tap into a glass
of home brew or boil the kettle for a warm-up
snorter of hot whiskey, deplete your stocks
of heather honey, lemons, cloves.

Oh for the gift of eptitude. No task too big or small or awkward.
As nifty with a reciprocating saw as with a humble bradawl.
Adept at fitting unfamiliar widgets instinctively in place.
No ceiling, joist, masonry or quarry tile an impediment.
Marking out a rebated joint one day, knuckling down
to a cavity tray the next; checking the leak from a valve
spindle, then flush-mounting a socket outlet nearby.
Keeping the show on the road, the jets in the air,
the world's motor lubricated, its axis oiled; waving
aside the clients' plaudits, though their bafflement
is absolute when that guiding hand withdraws.
But by then their lives are set to rights: piped water
sourced again, heat coursing through radiators, the car's
smutty engine blasting off with rejuvenated smoothness.

Then wrapping up a job, settling the tools in
the metal box, folding paint-drooled drop-cloths,
snapping the padlock back on the garden shed,
hosing down your splattered boots, changing
into a fabric-softened cotton polo shirt.
Even clicking the cap on the felt-tip, after
you sign off on the planning application.

Filing invoices, certificates, receipts
once the online tax form is completed
and the *Send* button flicked with relief.
Unwonted moments when all the pieces
cohere, loose ends tie up, quandaries resolve.

HEAD OFFICE

Gingham boxers. Toiletries.
Off-duty jeans. Workout tee-shirt, shorts.
Tablet loaded with the files
the showdown with the local unions
will require; stats to back up sobering
disclosures; an update on rebranding plans;
the latest on outsourcing routine maintenance.

How do they find the time to pack?
When does their schedule permit
a window in which they can be measured
for those slim-fit, lilac-striped shirts
matched with jacquard silk ties;
the smart, hand-crafted suits
no one would confuse with
scruffy off-the-peg stuff
middle managers luxuriate in:
chainstore shirts with buttoned
cuffs, half-pressed concertinaed
trousers sweeping the ground?

And when do they snatch the chance
to top up that stand-out tan – keepsake
of some beachfront villa break – that glows
in defiance of all rumours of low market
expectations, negative consumer sentiment?

It's that hour of evening when they
touch down at the airport in time to dine
with a joint venture partner, make a start
on the interim trading statement, review

next day's arrangements, text home, fire off
an ass-kicking circular to marketing staff.

Stand well back. Here one comes, shooing away
the taxi change, grabbing the wheeled
bag in one firm hand, the other ensuring
the cellphone's unbroken flow, then – ignoring
the bellhop's proffered cart – breezing past
the top-hat-doffing doorman to the carrara
marble lobby and the check-in desk where –
the still-vocal mobile shouldered now –
a gold card is extracted from the ID wallet's clutch.

SYNOPSIS

Life passes at a breakneck rate.
Brisk as text messages.
Time only for the executive summary.
The Dummies' Guide.
The podcast highlights.

The quick synopsis.
The cursory look.
The celeb gossip.
The abridged audiobook.
The no-frill stats. The FAQs.

Reading on a need-to-know basis.
Tweets of Breaking Sports News.
The World at a Glance
in the commuter freesheet.
History a volley of bullet points.

EXHIBITION

How would you like him done
as he roasts on his spit, taking the brunt
of the afternoon heat, skewers
gouging his hands and feet?

How exactly do you like him served?
Rare? – lance-pierced, oozing
maroon juices. Flambéed so fiercely
that no blush of butchery remains?

Do you take illicit pleasure in seeing him
finally nailed down – a bird of paradise;
an exotic death's-head moth,
arms outstretched like spindly wings?

Are you not altogether sorry to watch him,
rigid as a board with fear, tasting
his own medicine, sampling
the pain he added as standard –

with no convincing apologia –
to the human package deal?
Can you bear to catch him squirming,
bursting at the thoracic seams,

flesh vented with gashes, flensed,
the fractured laths of his rib cage
glued with blood as, subdued by
a centurion, he lies in his bed of nails?

Do you favour a script, like
a suicide note, above his head,
sending him up as *King of the Jews*?
Or would you let the scene

speak for itself, as a motley crew
of gawkers, spear-toting soldiers,
and his own blue-gowned
retinue sink to their knees?

Ought he to sleepwalk the plank
into the unknown? Or make his
escape like a contortionist,
reprieved nepotistically

by a *deus ex machina*?
Should you let him go hang,
exercising his free will to embrace
his plan with open arms?

Or, man to man, must you talk him
out of his grotesque death,
grant him your pardon,
commute his sentence to life?

AUTUMN

after Rainer Maria Rilke

Yielding to their frigid nature,
the weeks turn hard as frost.

The dayglo summer-registered liner
drifting serenely past – blue sky

an unflappable flag of convenience –
faces into choppy waters laced with ice.

Wrap the granite sundial in velvet
shadow. Let loose the winds:

release them back into the wild,
awarding them the freedom

of the planet, room for manoeuvre
under porous windows, doors.

Let the word on the grapevine
speak of essences: glutinous

fruit whose case is pressed
into red wine, condensing

summer's exuberance in a cask.
Those without a home will

never put down roots now,
building hopes on flimsy cardboard,

taking cold comfort from a bridge's
solid roof; it is too late in life's

season to contemplate a fresh start.
And the lonely – drafting lengthy,

unsent letters – adjourn sleep;
or walk the streets in no

particular direction, damp leaves
dogging their feet at every step.

REVENUE CUSTOMS

1 *Choir*

Let's hear it for the Revenue Choir, always
in place for the Tuesday night rehearsals,
putting a brave face on their way of life
irrespective of the vagaries of compliance rates,
lending grace notes to their line of work
whose clientele is never less than rancorous.

Listen as – after a shaky start – they bond
together in one voice, forging a harmony that
brings rapport between the contralto from
Large Cases and the bass from Prosecutions,
striking a note the Tax Credits expert
seconds, adding his full-throated support.

Give them a big hand, ladies and gentlemen,
whether at the Christmas concert, raising
the roof in aid of the homeless – who eke out
a life below poverty line, tax threshold –
or singing the praises of Handel and Bach
at the annual Mass for deceased staff.

Sometimes at end of day, filing
your papers away, exiting from
spreadsheets, flagging tomorrow's
priorities on your electronic diary.

Sometimes at end of day, when
the office eases into off-duty mode
and unfinished business – tricky
queries, constituency lobbying,
Ombudsman appeals – is put on hold:
network records backed-up,
plastic water pitcher communing
with its cooler, the row of corporate logos
watchful on the open-plan PCs.

Sometimes, at times like these,
they come to mind: old friends
and colleagues; bosses who were
sticklers for detail; dexterous drafters
of sub-sections, pluggers of loopholes;
custodians of the frosted public hatches;
income tax staff inured to tonguelashes;
larger-than-life characters – long dead –
who live on in these museum rooms.

Officers whose squashed initials
left their marks on carbon-copy letters
in archived files, who ruled these
marbled-papered daybooks now on show.
Staff who served at prefab border stations
or made landside seizures
of contraband at airport exit channels.

And sometimes at end of day,
the silence probes so deep
it proves an audit of official lives,
the years from shyly signing
entry papers in the Personnel Branch
to the long-service presentation by the Board.

Years showcased here, impressed in wax,
crystallised in glass, enshrined in paper,
pewter, brass: the past saved for the future,
like a budget surplus; not excised from
the record, but salvaged like scorched ledgers
from our war-torched Custom House.

III *Retirement*

I lost command of the integrated taxation system,
reconstructions and amalgamations legislation,
CGT multipliers, consanguinity reliefs. And there
petered out the susurrus of washroom gossip,

corridor banter, quick rejoinders capping my remarks.
Gone too the ecstasy of Friday evenings
every worker knows, the chastening
diminuendo that crept up on Sunday nights.

I forfeited my rightful place at the tea-break table.
An *I'm Boss* mug expectorating on the draining board.
The *Man United* one Tipp-Exed with a name.
A plastic milk container on which *Stats* is scrawled.

And I waived my advance access to the tax
defaulters list; confidential briefings on
exchequer trends; end-of-year appraisals;
clashes over heating levels, window openings.

Ten minutes fast, to trick me into rushing for
the morning bus, my hall clock was turned back
at last and could start living in the present,
its fidgety hands biding their time, not ushering

in the future any sooner than they strictly must.
My weary briefcase, facing redundancy from
leather fatigue, was relieved of further burdens.
I watched it – *I shall miss thee, Ariel* – wriggle from my grip.

After forty years, I could nearly hold the place
in my affections, look back lovingly at my
metal coat rack, take my last swig of the view
down the corridor's narrow undercroft

almost ruefully, leaving my office gutted –
cabinets in bits, cut-up desk borne
solemnly to a skip – creating space
for my successor to accommodate.

STILL

I know my type.
And I'm not impressed.
Throwbacks to an earlier age.
Set in our ways.
Getting more retro-looking every year.

Our dress code is old hat.
Our interest in networking sites is zilch.
Creatures of habit, we still insist
on written confirmations,
hard-copy documents.

Still hanker after printouts,
passbooks, cheques when
all about us bank online.
Still look to a wristwatch for the time.
Peruse the smudgy broadsheets for our news.

Spoilers of the nation's
vibrant image, its youthful
gung-ho status, here on
sufferance, surviving
past our die-before-date,

we fool no one with
our claims to feel
first rate, thank God.
Not a bother. Tip-top shape.
Touch coffin wood.

OUR FATHER

And we said unto God
'We adore you.'
> Stony silence.
> Cold shoulder.

And we added unto God
'We worship you.'
> Another brush-off.
> Further snubbing.

So, upping the ante
even more, we laid it on,
tried 'glorify' for size,
put 'venerate' to the test,
went all out, stretching
in sheer desperation
to our nuclear option,
proffering our ace card:
the heart-on-sleeve
one. intimating 'love'.
> Not a crumb of comfort
> from stale manna
> was lobbed back; not a
> tacit acknowledgement,
> a form letter.

Changing our tune then,
we picked up the old refrain:
'Our Father who art in heaven . . .'
> Though we put his own encomium
> where our mouths are,
> took it verbatim from

his book, this goodwill
gesture was made in vain.

'You alone are the most high'
we ventured next, relying
on this flattering strategy
to win us a reprieve.

       Yet every bid for conversation
       openers foundered:
       he was all take,
       no give – aloof, withdrawn,
       lacking social graces,
       a dead-loss at small talk,
       autistic in the distance
       he maintained.

His more needy hangers-on
hoped to read some esoteric
meaning in his silence.
'He moves in mysterious ways'
sufficed as formula
to mollify the docile types.
'The meaning is in the waiting'
a Welsh sceptic ventured.
'What does not reply is
the answer to prayer'
an English scribbler opined.

'Not my will, but thine be done'
boosted the next test rocket
we launched into his space
– more in hope than
expectation by that stage.

       And, true to form, not once
       did he engage, not once
       repent his stand-off.

                    As though some feud
                    among our families raged.

One millennium succeeded
another, without a thaw in this
cold war between the worlds;
no rapprochement of any
moment was forthcoming.

We were left no option but
to put the best interpretation
that we could on whatever
message was conveyed
by the attention-grabbing
voicemail he recorded
on day one: an opening
gambit that came out
of nowhere, bang
in the middle of nothing,
kicking up so vast a racket
we detect its background
music to this day, still treat it
as our sacred hymnal,
our foundational text,
a murmur from his bleeding
heart, as we peruse
the small print of atoms,
molecules, nanoparticles,
ruminate on lurid
supernova illustrations,
the illuminated manuscripts
of galaxies, over which lovers
pore in the dark nights
of their infatuated souls.

VALENTINE

Pure gravy. And don't forget it.
— RAYMOND CARVER

Back in hospital on this fateful date,
but to no complications for once,
I am discharged in good time to light
a candle on the kitchen table, decant
your Valentine's glass of sparkling wine,
sear the steak, sauté the onions, bake
potatoes till their paunchy waistcoats loosen,
launch the gravy boat on its salt voyage,
let mushrooms set sail on melting butter.

Life comes up trumps tonight:
a benchmark moment that we hope
to replicate; a precedent to ease us
through the testing times ahead;
a recipe for disaster aversion.
We note how simple its ingredients are,
yet how infrequently they coincide
in a single season, rare as love
enduring at millionth sight.

We rehearse its elements to
ourselves, like blessings counted,
rounding them up the way friends,
plotting a surprise party, will begin
accumulating mixers, napkins, dips for canapés . . .
Or as a hopeless man, laying down
furtive plans, might jealously
hoard pills, weedkiller, rope.

TESTS

What matters in this heartland
is the impression my chest
makes on the recording
angel's x-ray plate.

I am the colour of my sputum.
The composition of my mid-flow urine.
The density of my bones, made
irrefutably known through MRI.

The scrapings of blood that open
the floodgates to analysis
of my most revealing traits,
spill my deepest secrets.

Death begins to seem a feasible
proposition, a viable option.
I start to look the part, meet the job spec:
age; constitution; medical track record.

Everything proceeds apace:
I might be an executive shortlisted
for a company directorship,
the hot tip in the race for CEO.

I am ready to throw my hat
into the ring, fill my parents' shoes,
follow in a family tradition that
goes back as far as can be traced.

FAIR GAME

The elephant in the room
is sick of being ignored,
presumed too thick-skinned
to have feelings of its own.

It raises its trunk in protest
like a megaphone: a corrugated
tube to amplify its message,
trumpet its urgency.

But the hall threatens to erupt.
Who allowed this cretin entry?
How did a beast so monstrous
squeeze into this conference space?

Should Security not have seized
its cutthroat tusks outside?
This ghastly animal must be sent
packing, dumped in the nearest jungle.

Get this elephant out of the room.
A show of hands will be enough to lend
the motion force: *Let there be no free*
speech for outlandish species here.

THE POWER AND THE GLORY

God's coffers have run low,
now that so many litigants sue
for restitution, demand redress.

He stands charged with misdeeds
of the utmost gravity: he let his garden
run to seed, neglected to purge it of bad

apples, failed to flush them from his ranks
for gross depravity, ignored equality legislation,
displayed no modicum of *noblesse oblige*,

never delivered on the commitments
set out, chapter and verse, in his
gold-edged, calfskin-bound manifestos.

Instigator of a terror campaign,
dating from time immemorial,
he inflicted death on every creature

he had brought to life: a massacre
of innocents, a planetary genocide.
His actions come back to haunt him now.

His record is open to criminal inquisition,
his underworld connections questioned.
His own judgement day has arrived.

We were hungry, but you didn't deign
to break our fast, his lapsed followers
chant; we were thirsty, they croak,

yet not a bead of water rinsed our throats.
We went down on our knees
and pleaded with you – to no avail:

we were expected to survive on a wing
and a prayer, thrive on parables, beatitudes,
pious aspirations, mystifying aperçus;

promissory notes that might be
redeemed at some unspecified
time, some arbitrary last day.

You were all talk, never practised what you
preached, disinherited the meek, hinted at
a second coming, to keep us permanently tractable.

You have been top dog too long,
corrupted by your absolute power,
too habituated to the perks of high office,

at odds with the assumptions of a democratic
age when even a god should mix and mingle
more, prove a dab hand at crisis management,

speak in tongues lay people understand,
cut the arcane jargon of theology, cease
talking down, citing scripture for every purpose,

meting out the silent treatment to those
brave souls who challenge your behaviour.
No wonder your fan base dwindles

to a handful, your poll ratings plummet
to an all-time low: congregations, voting
with their feet, desert your sinking barque.

Enough of your prima donna stuff.
Enough of your cult of personality.
Enough of your craving for acclaim.

Enough of lapping up our worship.
Enough of tripping on our sycophantic hymns.
Enough of fishing for our compliments.

Enough of your divine right to rule.
Enough of foisting benign interpretations
on your unconscionable behaviour.

Enough of your surveillance of our minds, while
purporting to have fitted mankind with free will,
your graven image covering a multitude of sins.

PECKING ORDER

Numbers in decline,
      dawn choruses manage
with more modest forces
      like authentic performances of Bach.

A one-for-sorrow magpie,
      rough diamond, on the grass.
And two greenfinches:
      consolation enough.

How dainty the wren's
working parts must be.

How elfin the furnace
that keeps its heart warm.

How miniature the brain-chip
which triggers its alarm.

Drop everything.
The blackbird – jewel on
the crown of the chimney cowl –
must be granted a fair hearing,
afforded the last word.

NOT THE DEAD

It is not the dead who haunt us.
There is no further damage they can do.
We have seen them to death's door.

Made sure they had expired.
Double-checked their pulse.
Tested them for livor mortis, breath.

Turned them over to embalmers
who stitched their lips.
Left them deaf and dumb.

Burned them to a cinder.
Buried them up
to their oxters in muck.

It is the not-yet-born
we are up against.
They will be the first to forget us.

Strike down our judgements
as null and void.
Rewrite our history.

Consign us to the past.
Find solutions to what baffled us.
Put us down to experience.

Outlast us.

TIME ENOUGH

The tally of years
added up so rapidly
it appeared I had
been short-changed,
tricked by sleight
of hand, fallen victim
to false bookkeeping.

Yet when I checked
my records, each
and every year had
been accounted for,
down to the last day,
and could be audited
against old diary entries
(client briefings,
dental check-ups,
parent-teacher meetings,
wedding anniversaries),
verified with credit
card statements
(multi-trip insurance,
antibiotics, concert bookings,
mobile top-ups).

And, although
nagging doubts
remained – an
inkling that I had
been ripped off
in some way,
given short shrift,

made to live at an
accelerated pace,
rushed through
my routines with
unseemly haste –
nothing could be proved,
no hard and fast
statistics adduced.

I had, it seems,
unknown to me,
been living my
life to the full.

THE BARK

The bark knows more than we do.
It is sticking to its story, yapping all night
with a conviction very like the truth,
a credible witness statement.

That bark goes back a long way: it is
on the trail of Odysseus's tail-flagged
homecoming, as the dying Argos tries
to raise his standard to its former mastery.

Replicated in fleabitten city slums,
reiterated on remotest farms, it spreads
rumour in the night hours, alarming
those who lie awake enumerating fears,

assuring them their troubles will
not pass, their heartaches, pains,
will not last one day less than a dog's
lifespan converted into human years.

Barks call us into question, pitch their
message at a level we can apprehend only
too well: they speak our inner language,
adopt the idiolect we use in self-address.

Days that demand a snarling riposte,
canines exposed. And days that fetch up
nowhere much to growl about.

Yet, faithful to its calling, the bark
remains on high alert at all times,
never lets its guard down.

THE FINGER

Allow us
this much,

at least,
as keepsake,

father – your
legacy to

a world
you snubbed,

stubbed out
so abruptly:

your cigarette-
stained

index finger
 ۱۱۱۱۱۱۱

in its sad
marinade

must still
remain in clay,

stuck in its
accusatory groove,

tanned by
your nervous

chain-smoker's
fumes, the way

an oak coffin
is treated with

a wood preservative
until fully cured.

THE LONG CORRIDOR

It was late when we chanced on the seminary.

Dark and wet and late. Windy, cold, forlorn.
Lights low. Not a soul to be seen, no candle
burning at either end of the long corridor.

The silence was the midnight ash sifting,
the ember-shifting stir in a presbytery grate.
The silence of pre-dawn meditation.

The incredulous silence that follows accusation
when the chilling message filters down the waxed
corridors of ears and a full confession is warranted.

❧

Processing against the currents of empty space,

we contemplate the scrubbed, smiling
Ordination Day faces on framed photographs,
numbers dwindling towards millennial zeroes.

Portrayed along the hall in holy oils, set forever
in their pious ways, prelates robed in princely satins,
Sunday best, are taken by surprise;

men at ease with talk of *magisterium*,
fides divina, who believed – in all
good faith – they served a sacred mission.

❧

Bare ruined choirs, labourers too few,
the seminaries drift nearer the abyss;
and in deconsecrated buildings, converted

to hotels, couples immerse themselves in
whirlpool spa, jacuzzi, or mortify the flesh
with weights and treadmills in the gym.

God is well and truly dead and buried,
his name no longer raised in polite company.
Mystery solved. Case closed.

꙳

High time, therefore, to leave the long corridor
– its wimpled lilies, its festering anemones –
to its own destiny, sad relic of another age.

Not the faintest ray, not the dimmest glimmer
of light, shines at the end of its tunnel
vision, not a glint of the infinite can be divined.

BLASTS

How come the winds of childhood
blow so fiercely, so insistently,
    still spill out their tales of woe?
You'd have thought they might
    have piped down long ago,
found someplace else to settle,
    something else to whine about,
given it a rest, stopped moving
    heaven and earth to underscore
their message, let off whatever
    head of steam had built up,
then made away for calmer latitudes.
    Instead, they regroup with new force,
roughing you up, calling your bluff,
    activating body searches,
triggering flashbacks, memory attacks
    that shatter your defences,
leave your self-esteem in tatters,
    bring your ramparts crashing down.
Just when you think their minds
    are sealed away with childish
things, kept under lock and key,
    sent to their rooms in deep
disgrace, placed under curfew,
    they drift downstairs and,
spoiling for a fight, recommence
    their bluster: dredging up old
horrors, insinuating blame,
    taunting you with backchat,
leaking secrets, blasting out
    transgressions from the past,
chanting schoolyard names.

SAY BUT THE WORD

You eat your ill-judged
      words in the early
hours, take them back,

retract them one by one,
      try to erase the memory,
remove all trace,

arrive at more benign
      interpretations:
some form of words

to set your stressed-out
      mind at rest,
broker a truce with

your unyielding self,
      allow you draft terms
you could sleep on,

leaving the record blank
      as the crumpled sheets
you toss between.

      ❦

Say the word 'Future':
      you despatch it to the past.

Say the word 'Silence':
      you undo it.

Say the word 'Nothing':
        you make something of it.

                        [*after Wislawa Szymborska*]

Phone home urgently.
        The power of simple words.
You never forget.

So many of the things
        we go in fear of most
may never happen.

We fear them all the more
        the more they keep
not happening.

Where there's life
there's hope.

Hope and despair.

Despair because
we can but hope.

A WORD

To set up house and home, share
bed and board, with a near-stranger
seems an improbable thing to do,
not least for loners like ourselves:

covetors of our own private space;
slow burners, not given – except
in irony – to extravagant endearments
and never to the demonstrativeness of

Valentine's Day deliveries to your workplace,
red-ribboned frivolities and padded cards.
Yet, by now, our understanding runs
so deep, we'd recognise each other

in our sleep and are sensitive
to the merest tonal fluctuations,
minuscule variations in mood,
permanently on the alert for the unsaid.

We charge summer sale bargains
to the same credit card; find ample
accommodation under one double sheet,
neither party yanking it too far

towards their own side; the porch's
long-life bulb aglow in winter, agog for
the arrival of whoever is the later home
to narrate the day's adventures;

communication so close we split
our colds between us equally, share
viruses like a joint bank account, a
comprehensive policy with 'named driver'.

So here we are, all these years later:
old-stagers of the kind we'd have been
quick to ridicule once, deride as
a couple too set in their ways,

presiding in near-silence over breakfast –
adjusting the coffee plunger, buttering
crunchy toast – with nothing at all
between them needing a word.

IMAGO

Somebody made in the image of a god granted us the benefit of his protection racket.

Someone answering to the name 'God' undertook, on the strictest possible conditions, to keep us from harm's way.

Some force, for which the word 'god' must suffice, stormed into town, promising the sun, moon and stars.

Some man of godlike stature gave us to believe there was nothing on earth – or heaven – we could not achieve.

Somebody purporting to be a god was ready to cut a deal on a time-share in eternity.

Some man with godly presence, adopting multiple aliases, turned up around the world, instilling hope and terror in the locals.

Some character claiming to be god's representative on earth, his sole agent, his authorised spokesman, snapped up votaries the way cash-for-gold shops amass their precious metals.

Some showman, up to his god-like tricks, on tour for a limited run only, mesmerised audiences with his antics: sea-striding, lacing tap water with best vintage, then genetically modifying the wine into his blood.

Some charismatic man, having stepped out of nowhere, relegated earth to a transit camp, dangled the prospect of permanent residency in his kingdom.

Some smooth talker, blessed with god-like confidence, trotted out his one-stop response to every mystery, the same pat explanation for every baffling facet of creation.

Some philanthropic figure who would pass for a god, basking in his offshore haven, backed by unlimited assets, was prepared to stand surety, procure eternal remission for good behaviour.

Someone omniscient enough to be a god pledged a further coming; but – time-span winding down, lamp oil running low – we fear we have been stood up, palmed off with this mystifying no-show.

HOW OLD THE YEAR

Summer's frivolousness, its *joie de vivre*,
its live-for-the-day impulsiveness,
gives way to darker moods.

The last of the bees, scoffing dregs
of nectar – shoppers with their
snouts in end-of-season bargain

troughs – have left the scene.
Swallows, like tax exiles, pack
for more lenient regimes.

Elderberries crushed for wine
are the broken blood vessels
in an ageing face.

Apples fatten into jams and jellies,
chestnuts in polished casing
are hauled over smoky coals.

Something chill begins to stalk
the land, proves itself a force still.
There is no going back now: too late

to stop the rot, resurface corroded
leaves, conserve them like the copper
fittings from some listed building.

An uncanny charge remains in
the space discarded by the songbird.
Condensation draws a veil across the glass.

You scratch about for things to do, change
the filter on the wintering lawnmower,
measure for extra shelving in the utility room.

The sun settles at a modest level,
its light on a dimmer switch, enters a less
frenzied phase, simmers in its own juices

like comfort food, a mutton and veg
concoction, stewing in a slow cooker,
for your homecoming from the wind-chilled dark.

Stars proliferate: sesame seeds
sprinkled at night on a bowl of oatmeal
set in readiness for a quick breakfast.

It is the time of lowered expectations,
long, unnerving silences, vitality slumps.
Night-class websites prompt old memories

of back-to-school resumptions, the tactile
pleasure of fresh textbooks, the rousing
smell of newness wafting from unsullied pages

How old and stiff the year looks, slowing
noticeably, showing its age, summer's
laughter lines wrinkling its rigid face.

Even the mightiest trees are ruffled: shaken
by the force of muscle-flexing gales, they drag
on their reluctant shadows, clinging for support.

Though chastened, less intense, the light can
still surprise, stepping unscathed from a great
weight of cloud; raising the day's stakes,

it comes down on the side of a field,
catches it unawares, places a possessive
finger on its ploughed-up ground,

offers no explanation for why this
should be the favoured one, allowed its
moment of pre-eminence in the sun.

THERE IS NO REASON

There is no reason they can tell
why this life should not go on for ever.
The unflagging adults bang about
already in the kitchen where the flypaper
is scored with victories over evil
and the sausage-spiced air
they could slice with that breadknife
sinking its serrated teeth
into a buttermilk-based raisin loaf
hisses as the frying pan's palm is greased
with newly-churned doubloons of gold.

Friesian cows top up with marginal grass
on rambling journeys to the milking
parlour's lactic whitewashed walls.
A stippled calf is on the loose
like a stray dalmatian pup.
Frantic hens scour the yard
for something they never mislaid.
The chubby sow slumped
in an armpit of mud, wallows
shamelessly in stained pink
nakedness, the full concatenation
of her tits on show.

Each day's routine is foreknown always.
Which field needs a fallow season. Which rotation.
When the seed potatoes should be planted.
When to risk the first nick in the meadow.
When the time is ripe for the combine
to make quick work of the corn.

Wisdom is a given, like the lush lime soil.
Like the climate which – for all their perennial whining –
gets it right on the whole, increasing (or not)
precipitation to the requisite extent,
turning up (or down) the volume of the sun
by the most appropriate degrees,
its tour de force their toast if it
delivers archetypal summer days,
hot on each other's heels, burning
with zeal to alchemise their crops.

Though not of this world, they know
full well each rood and perch they've
been allotted: its high points, its weak spots,
every vagary of its behaviour.

The last rounds of haycocks, raking in
the heat, sundried like sandcastles,
must be rushed away to the safe
haven of the barn in case the fragile
weather shatters into smithereens of rain.
Cattle – methodically grazing meadows,
not missing out on a single juicy shoot –
will be drenched against liver fluke and husk.

Wake up, children.
Get dressed. Fast.
Haven't you noticed it's morning?
A once-off morning, far too good to miss.
The sun has been casting about for ages,
raring to shadow your adventures all day long.

Be seated on the timber form
while your honey-sweetened oatmeal
cools and home-cured bacon
blossoms rosily on the pan.

THE FALL

The backyard wall
stands guard between me
and the cemetery
on the other side.

My garden haven
is a riot of colour,
red-hot pokers stoked
like flaming swords.

The far side is devoid
of life, headstones drab
as concrete slabs
of high-rise flats;

a living death: freedom
of expression is withheld,
travel rights suppressed;
scarcities abound.

Tenacious as a border
guard's alsatian,
ivy sinks its vicious
teeth into the wall:

its fall will force
a regime change,
unite me with
that darker side.

BEST PRACTICE

Dear God!
Oh man!
How did a being of your supreme intelligence
get bogged down in our affairs,
dragged to our mundane level,
entangled in our fate?

Was there an element
of repentance in your actions?
Having botched our prototypes,
betrayed our cosseted first parents,
placed temptation in their way,
and – with apple tree as plant –
acted as agent provocateur,
laid a honeytrap for Adam,
did a guilty conscience
bring you down to earth,
shocked that creatures
made in your own image
proved so fallible?

Were you hoping
to amend our ways,
ameliorate our faults,
attempt a product recall,
make ad hoc conversions
to our fallen natures,
patch up our shortcomings,
adapt us to best practice,
tweak our hardwiring,
energise our lives with love –
like some new biofuel – in lieu

of our more toxic kinds of power,
high-octane club and dagger hatreds,
our machete and Kalashnikov aggression?

You went to incredible lengths
to become one of us: stressing
how intensely you felt our pain,
knew what we endured daily.
But how convincingly did
you play this snivelling role?
Were you not badly miscast
in humble guise, as you tried
to flaunt your bona fides,
flourish your common humanity,
while – a populist president with
a Liechtenstein bank stash –
the best seat in your father's mansion
was reserved for you alone,
who never shared our fear
of the unknown, who were spared
our insecurity of tenure?

Spoiled rotten by your privileged lineage,
born with an apostle spoon in your mouth,
you failed to rein in your snobbier traits,
your petulant behaviour, incensed by
those who questioned your credentials,
stamping your sandalled foot, letting
us go to hell if we didn't live strictly
by your book; willing to forgive us,
turn the other cheek, provided of course
we surrendered on your terms,
meekly adhered to the dictates
you set in stone, threw ourselves
at your mercy, adopted your norms,

respected your dress code,
conformed to your sexual constraints,
conceded your hierarchy of sins.

Your coming among us was
a madcap charade, a reckless
prank allowed to go too far.
You planned your death
as the perfect crime,
expecting others to take the rap,
get caught in the act,
while you washed your hands
of guilt, though the perpetrators
were mere scapegoats,
more sinned against than sinning:
dupes who followed your orders,
fleshed out your script,
gave credence to your actions.
And then, to crown it all, weren't
you sighted three days later
like a life insurance fraudster
born again with a new identity?

Espousing peace and sword,
you were street angel
and house devil personified.
You charged your father
with forsaking you, yet lent
your imprimatur to his brand,
established your cross
as a global logo, promoting
the family firm, and obligingly
fulfilled a plethora of prophecies,
checking them off, balancing
the two books to marshal
their testaments into synch.

You wanted things
both ways at once.
To play lion and lamb.
To be God and man.

And were never
more vulnerable,
never more
lovably human,
than in that
dithering spirit.

MEMOIR

It has been
absolutely

fascinating
being me.

A unique
privilege.

Now my
whole life

lies ahead
of you.

No thanks
at all are

called for,
I assure you.

The pleasure
is all mine.

PAPER TRAIL

Once, money had credibility. Its word was its bond.
The story it told was backed up by casket-shaped gold bullion
interred in cold, calculating vaults of central banks.

Once, money added up, was secure in its identity, knew
exactly what it stood for. It had standing: was seed capital,
buying power, providence, a healthy reserve for future needs.

The love of money was the root of evil. Yet thrift was virtuous.
Saving was good for the soul. The poor would always be with
    you.
You gave to God and Caesar, took whatever credit you were
    due.

Prudence was guaranteed. Fixed returns on principal assured.
Old money was deferred to, its ancestry traced to slavery,
hard labour, patented inventions, plantation estates.

The money trail led to the bank's rock-solid door: time locks,
safe deposits, a manager preaching restraint, making you pay
for your excesses, demanding deeds to underwrite his trust.

Then the bottom line turned notional; losses, gains
proved mere statistics, collateral for loans a default mode
consigned to timorous, wimpish, bygone times.

Labyrinthine instruments were trafficked on
global exchanges in the blink of a cursor's eye,
quicker than a bullish broker could roar 'Buy!'

Every big deal was a bonus for the Lamborghini-owning trader
playing the markets who (such heady discretion, such adrenalin!),
with a click of the finger, could drive his pedimented institution
    to the wall.

Now where does the paper trail – demented treasure hunt –
lead? When you follow the money, you are directed down
a dirt road that denies you purchase on its slippery surface.

You are on your own. Press onward? Abandon route?
Who knows? The silence, like a bubble, tightens hold.
Some miscalculation made has led you down this path.

STOCKS

while stocks fail
like blighted crops

your best investment
for a steady yield

a return guaranteed each year
is a field of grain

ears braided
like a pony's mane

sheaves of frantic grasses
easily swayed

but calmer when
a dose of drowsy

poppy blossoms
is dispensed

or risk a flutter
on a herd

of butter-sculpted
cows grazing

near a stream
from which foam

rises to the top
like cream:

crush market
forces with

a cloven hoof
a cheddar wheel

SNOW

Snow has sentimentalised the world,
       left it sugar-coated, a baked alaska
conjured from the palest of vanilla ice creams,
       the purest of swan's egg whites,
its mushy, too-sweet-to-be-wholesome look
       topped with a confection of candied trees –
bare-branched candelabras – holly waxing
       eloquent with berries in a citric winter dusk.

In denial about whatever smacks of negativity,
       it stops death in its tracks, adopts a hard
line on burials, sets up road blocks, brings runways
       to a standstill, placing travel plans on ice,
permitting no escape from its airbrushed vision,
       plotting to frustrate communications
networks, keep bad news in abeyance, seal
       the mouth of every outlet, stifle all dissent.

Its powder washes whiter than any rival's,
       outshines the field blanching moon's,
obliterates earth's lumpy surfaces, smoothes
       its awkward bumps, insists simplicity is truth.
Too good to last, too huge a con-job
       to sustain, too false a façade
to maintain beyond one season, snow's
       hour of reckoning comes, its defences

crumble like a pomegranate meringue
       gateau, churning mucky sludge,
a filthy vinegar of meltwater under which
       the world it wished away can be defrosted,

dust itself off, when spring's no-nonsense air
          prevails: its new twig broom will sweep
all vestiges of slush before it, letting life resume
          its complex, messy, necessary routines.

DEAR LIFE

you should be the love of my life,
my soulmate, the entire
raison d'être of my existence.

I have devoted my whole life
to your cause, doing my utmost
to stay in your good books,

keep on your right side, humour
you with guff about how truly
wonderful you are: a miracle;

the nest egg in which
I sank my hopes,
invested my life's savings.

ᔈ

Impulsive, prone to whim,
more than capable of turning
against me without just rationale,

you have proved a difficult match.
Yet there are times, life, when we
seem sublimely partnered and I yield

to mawkish talk: losing the run
of myself, I start to blab about us
sharing the remainder of our days.

ᔈ

Life gives
        us something
to live for:
        we will do
whatever it takes
        to make it last.
Kill in just wars
        for its survival.
Wolf fast-food
        during half-time breaks.
Wash down
        chemical cocktails,
as prescribed.
        Soak up
hospital radiation.
        Prey on kidneys
at roadside pile-ups.
        Take heart
from anything
        that might
conceivably grant it
        a new lease.
We would give
        a right hand
to prolong it.
        Cannot imagine
living without it.

⁊

And we go to
      the ends of the earth
to further life's ideals,
      build on overgrazed
savannah blades,
      lop down
forest canopies,
      dole out supplies
of nylon tents
      to famine refugees,
purify our sewage,
      drink recycled piss,
having issued
      lesser species with
notice to quit,
      driven them underground,
sent them scurrying
      into oblivion,
stuffed them for
      museum displays,
glad to see the tail end
      of their ruddy butts,
thuh tuaic fungr,
      their shitty scuts,
regretting only the loss
      of ivory supplies,
aphrodisiacal rhino horns.

           ~

Life is a full-time role,
its terms and conditions
as tricky to get your
mind around as rules

of foreign grammars:
mastering its usages with
native speaker fluency
requires constant practice.

And it goes beyond a joke
as you grow to comprehend
the full extent of the
obligations laid at your door:

Save the planet. Cut back
on plastic packaging.
Shield your children
from chatroom predators.

Buy fairtrade fruit.
Love thy neighbour:
rein in your impulse
to beat him to a pulp.

Refrain from counterfeit
designer fashions,
defamation. Indulge all
things in moderation:

sex, embezzlement, booze.

Tossed together out of stellar stuff,
deposited on a hostile planet, left
to fend for our perishable selves,

pick up the entire tab – the total
cost of living – as though the onus
fell entirely on our shoulders,

we reap and sow for our survival –
runner beans, asparagus, mango,
whatever current climatic conditions

allow – plant tea on terraced hills
steam-cleaned in a brew of pristine
mist, try to make sense of our plight,

look to the star-crossed sky at night
for leads, trace the sparkle in an eye
to the cosmic soot and sand wedged

between the constellations, then track
the orbit of our ancestry down to earth,
track upon the fossil record where

an ur-parent slithers out of its allotted
habitat, worms its way from the sea
on thin, fin-like transparent props:

gasping like a transatlantic wave
collapsing at its final landing place,
it transmogrifies into our futures here,

equips us to cap oil spills, propagate
GM crops, foil teenage cybercrime, cope
with information overload, age-old disease.

Poorly adapted to the hazards
of the world, we don crash helmets
to soften impacts, our torsos
strapped to car seats for safekeeping,
heat borrowed from bedclothes,
sweaters, woodchip stoves,
always privileging our own lives,
keeping our digestive juices
flowing at any cost, even as
our prime is well behind us,
time stiffening its arthritic resolve
as we cling to dwindling existences
by walking frames, lean on
the acquiescing shoulders
of crook-handled canes,
help just a panic-button away
so that we can fend off
the death from which the breezy
medics shelter us, although it
goes on festering under our
noses, our cataract-blurred eyes.

No disrespect to death, but it meddles
too much with the living, ordering them about,
tormenting the life out of the able-bodied,
lodging bullet-sized tumours in soft tissue,
flooring the unwary with an underhand attack,
its one-track mind focussed on ambushing
its victims, picking them off like a serial killer
waging a personal vendetta, its bony finger
beckoning the unsuspecting baby
to its cot death, insisting the hour
of reckoning has come for the military chief
and the grief counsellor, diverting people
from whatever plans they've made, subverting
their potential to its own monomaniacal aims,
blowing them off course as though they had
sold their bodies in some diabolical pact
and the moment of truth – payback time –
had come to pass, undermining their
confidence in the future, dictating their fate,
altering conditions of service in mid-contract,
suffering life to carry on without them.

.🐄

And after your parents'
Big Bang, here you stand;
you can do no other: too remote
a creation to be fathomed
even by yourself, but emitting
distant signals that attest
positively to your existence.
It is no easy station to be
assigned: inhabiting your own
space, knowing you will
collapse in on yourself,
and conscious, mean time,
of the dark matter you contain,
the dark energy that rages
in your sphere, the infernos
seething beneath the crust of skin
that constitute your very core.

Incapable of grasping a fraction
of the scientific data – the latest
takes on leptons, quantum
theory, gravitational entropy –
so much of which remains
above our heads, generating
more heat than light, we feel
weighed down with its gravity,
prefer to be left in the dark,
reduce the mesmerising
revelations to a human scale,
happily distracted by more
mundane stuff, try to reconstruct
the case for our preeminent
status as a species, recall
the whys and wherefores
of our special destiny,
making up rules as we go along
that harden into rituals
and laws, become elevated
to dogmas, superstitions,
myths, our assumptions
adopted as immutable truths,
our nobler and our baser traits
fractured into warring factions,
throwing body and soul into
the fray, one half living for
the dwindling day, the other
laying claim to notions of eternity.

~~

Finally, I cracked life's code, bored straight into the nuclear core of its mystery. But having no paper to hand, I seized a newly-fallen autumn leaf, sketched my findings on its palm, not reckoning with the pilfering wind that snatched it from my grasp. Leaves swirl around my feet now in a crinkled tin-foil din. Thousands of leaves. A sybil's mixed signals, they shift positions, shuffle their decks like tarot packs, gyrate suggestively. I go on my knees in search. Keep on drawing blanks.

Thanks a heap, parents.
Your role in brokering my life proved vital:
you gave me heart and kidneys,
kitted me out with all the parts
I needed to assemble a full
working specimen of humanity.
Without your selfless organ donations,
how could I have known
how 'loneliness' is spelled,
gained insider knowledge of euphoria,
experienced the piquancy of mixed
emotions (pride in my children's
progress, say, allied to despair
of the future), learned to mow grass,
cook *al dente* pasta, etch a message
on train window condensation,
wait in a frigid church porch for
the hearse to emanate through rain,
report to Radiology
in my tartan dressing gown?
Muchas gracias, parents.
You were far too kind.
Where would I be without you?
You shouldn't have.

᪲

Nothing is beyond our understanding.
We will unravel all the secrets
of the universe for sure, tease out
the machinations that set the whole
shebang in perpetual motion, gave rise
to spiral galaxies, planetary rings,
antimatter, moonstruck oceans.

We launch telescopes to screen
archival footage: old clips replay
the initial flint sparks of existence;
capture the razzmatazz that marked
creation's opening phase, firework
displays that touched off the inaugural
torches: eternal flames.

Everything is under control:
curvaceous as planetary spheres,
the nicely-rounded figures
(distances, light years) are reeled off
confidently by cosmologists,
backed up by dusty ranks
of blackboard calculations.

Yet it can be lonesome this
far out on evolution's path:
no ultimate destination agreed;
no ecstatic ending guaranteed;
no Yggdrasil, no Dantean dark
wood in sight, for shelter on
this exposed stretch of road.

And miles to go. And miles to go.

You know full well the struggle
nought availeth, know you are
duped, lulled into a stupor
by so much willing diversion:
drown your winter sorrows in
a steaming chowder, follow
the squabbles at the bird feeder,
relive your hour of glory on reality TV,
the ace goal that changed the fortunes
of your street league team . . .
Nothing whatsoever you have
done, won, accomplished – your
personal best – will add up when
your final balance sheet is filed,
no matter how persuasively you
spoke on some Toastmasters motion,
how sportingly you stayed the course
in the mothers' egg and spoon race.
Whether you were decorated by some
pretender deemed to be your king,
or did time in the sex offenders' wing,
you will not escape with your life,
despite taking the necessary steps
to pass on the essence of this venture –
doomed as it is – to future generations,
initiate them in your doubtful ways.

It's good on the whole
to be bypassed by life,
not thrust into the limelight
or the firing line, but not
forgotten either; dropped in on
intermittently – an ivied
abbey accessed through
a plashy field; an obscure
website registering a few hits.

꒜

Demand for human life is soaring.
Projections for the coming decades
forecast unprecedented growth,
the scale so great, migration
of souls so commonplace, no one
can keep an accurate track.

Ganging up on hegemonic death,
our numbers must surpass
the skull-count of the all-time dead.
It only takes a few minutes to make
a man, a late 'Dream Song' maintains,
laying it on the line, but exaggerating

the case, when less than seconds –
teenage haste, spontaneous urge –
will do the needful consummately.
End-result the same in terms of hungers
to feed, feelings not to hurt, bereavement
counselling to dispense, convictions to appeal.

꒜

Where did it go, that life
I once held firmly in my
grasp, heart fluttering
in eagerness, suspense;

fluttering like a bird
trapped between palms
before striking out for freedom
and wide open skies?

You have reached the postscript stage,
left just enough room on the thin-skinned
page to allow you set the record straight
(that one moral collapse, that single lapse
of judgement scarring you for life),
put the best construction possible
on your past, lend your behaviour
a more favourable slant, avail of this
breathing space to deflect attention
from your gaffes, spare your blushes,
permit some, at least, of your redeeming
features to be credited, before – too late –
you fizzle out into ellipses and your
life is designated a done deal.

Dear death,
we were destined
to meet sooner or later.
Now I've come to be
your understudy,
monitoring my regress
towards your ends.

Dear friends, you owe
a debt of gratitude to me.
There was a need,
statistically speaking,
for this diagnosis
to be pinned on
somebody, like blame.

So be glad it was *my*
name that was called,
my number that was
up, that it is to me
it falls to satisfy
the quota. And let this
be my legacy to you:

I saved your lives.

When the results
came through,
I was no less alive.

Alive enough to know
the score. As alive
as the woman giving birth

in the top-floor ward.
As alive as the wailing
outcome of her labours.

As alive as the partisan
young man sniping at a
US convoy; the teenage DJ

deafening neighbours;
the broker notching up
another killing on utilities.

To buy a pair of shoes
was an act of faith
in my own prospects.

When I paid a bill,
my spending too
boosted consumer trends.

My referendum vote
counted just as much
as anyone's.

This was life
more or less
as I had known it.

I caught an inkling of resistance
from the corner
of the mirror's eye.

And when my stomach
grumbled, it was for
life itself it hungered.

ADMISSIONS

Before you do down life again,
badmouth a world that never lives up
to its billing, recall how glorious it seemed,
your unwillingness to let go, that evening
you were driven to Admissions.

Every shabby sight you passed
gleamed with some ameliorating
feature, mustering enough initiative
to demonstrate its best case scenario.
Your own scrawny excuse for a lawn –

one part weed to two parts moss –
glowed with previously unsuspected
zest; the day's remaining light was fraying
at the edges as the sun signed off on
the horizon's dotted line: a virtuosic chef,

concocting dishes from leftovers,
drizzling pigment, tossing in whatever
mix of clashing tinctures lay unused.
How carefree everyone appeared as
they flashed momentarily into view

along your painful route: tourists perusing
the early-bird menu, a buggy-wheeling
mother cutting through church grounds,
hoodies ganging up against the counter
in the steamy comfort of the takeaway.

That you fell for the world's seductive looks
that evening in the psychedelic dusk
is not to be denied; how some confidence –
insider information you had withheld until then –
was let slip: *and he saw that it was good.*

NOCTURNE OP. 2

A sad air's best for night as you mope about
the house, closing windows, checking doors.
Slow, cumulative strokes of the violin bow,
the most ruminative notes that can be coaxed
from the cello, nocturnes unlocked by black piano keys.

Strains that are trained directly on the heart
when its resistance sinks, like temperatures,
to a day's-end low: music that tells of how
things stand in the troubled world you now have
in your hands to potter about in on your own.

Music of the kind whose fearful darkness would
unnerve you as a child, but whose darkness
seems the very point, this late night here; a slow
movement's stark conclusions ringing sadly true.

Some new and recent poetry from Anvil

NINA BOGIN
The Lost Hare

NORMAN CAMERON
Collected Poems and Selected Translations
Edited by Warren Hope and Jonathan Barker

PETER DALE
Diffractions
New and Collected Poems

JENNIE FELDMAN
Swift

HARRY GUEST
Some Times

JAMES HARPUR
Angels and Harvesters

NICHOLAS KILMER
Petrarch: Songs and Sonnets

GABRIEL LEVIN
To These Dark Steps

E A MARKHAM
Looking Out, Looking In
New and Selected Poems

ALAN MOORE
How Now!

JULIAN TURNER
Planet-Struck

NASOS VAYENAS
The Perfect Order
Selected Poems
Edited by Richard Berengarten and Paschalis Nikolaou

www.anvilpresspoetry.com